THE STORY OF DESIGN

THE STORY OF
DESIGN

MARION DOWNER

Lothrop, Lee and Shepard Co. Inc. ⚬ New York

Contents

"Whatever we look at with delight,
whatever we see that gives us pleasure,
though we may think we have forgotten it the next day
—will influence us all our lives."

George Santayana

DESIGN

its universal use and purpose

Figure of a horse. White jade. China, Ch'ing dynasty, 1662–1722. Metropolitan Museum of Art

Design is the expressive shaping of contours and the decorative spacing of an area into parts.

Linen and wool textile. Spain, 16–17th century. Cooper Union Museum

Ice floes. Woodcut by Peter Sager. Canada, contemporary. Philadelphia Museum of Art

A design can express a thought, a feeling.

But its greatest purpose is to give enjoyment.

Linen panel, embroidery in wools. England, late 16th century. Cooper Union Museum

DESIGN BEGINNINGS

*today's view
of a far-distant past*

A bear and a bird. Carved amber. Viking region, 8000 to 5000 B.C. National Museum of Denmark

So long ago that there is no history to tell us of their lives, men carved these little forms in amber. Even the exact place where they were found is now unknown.

Designers from the mysterious past are nameless but it is clear that, with their tools of sharpened stone, they could slant and curve the contours of the things they made in ways that show expressive shaping.

They worked, unconscious of artistic rules. Design was as they felt it.

At the time this vase was painted, the ice age had ended and great areas of Africa were left dry and barren.

Here we see rows of moving animals on their way to better pastures along the Nile, a decorative design that tells of a man's dream of good hunting. The Nile was indicated by repeated wavy lines in loops at upper left and right.

To paint a thought, to tell a story with a brush! It was easier than talking, better than weaving a basket out of colored straws.

Pottery jar, decorated with gazelles and ostriches. Egypt, pre-dynastic, before 5000 B.C. Metropolitan Museum of Art

The designs made by the straws in woven baskets had great interest for design-conscious primitive men. Sometimes a piece of pottery would be made by lining a basket with a layer of clay pressed tightly inside, then putting it in fire to bake. The straws burned and disappeared, but a hardened pot that bore their marks was left.

The rotund vessel shown here may have been formed and decorated in that way. It has what might be called artless beauty.

Earthen vessel with handles and markings. Region of Denmark, about 2700–2300 B.C. National Museum of Denmark

Ornament that was consciously designed often consisted merely of painted bands, happily varied in width and spacing. On this vase there were added a number of small round decorations.

Such circles—or symbols—were the designed answer to primitive man's natural questions about the origin of life, of life within life—or beyond it.

Amphora. White painted pottery. Cyprus, early iron age, from 1000 B.C. Metropolitan Museum of Art

Life as he found it is expressed by the designer of this cup. He was content to express his own experience. But grace of contour was important, and the space divisions in the strip around the top were made with an eye for balance.

Unskilled designers usually covered completely the surface to be decorated. Here, some of the space has purposely been left empty to allow emphasis to be put on the animal.

The animal is strangely drawn, but truthfully—if the designer's intention was to express a listening, cautious step. And the direction of that step is continued in a dipping line painted on the base of the cup.

All space is really in use. That is design.

Pottery cup. Unglazed terra cotta. Iran, 3000 B.C. Metropolitan Museum of Art

It was design to shape this useful object with pleasingly balanced contours. It was design to contrast a decorated area with a plain one—burnished to show its golden beauty.

Circles in the gold were arranged to make a rhythmic pattern which was natural in the land where it was made—the Mesopotamian Valley. It was there that some mathematician established the measurement of the circle into 360 degrees and the hour into 60 minutes.

Geometry, visualization, design.

Gold ewer. Height 7 inches. Ancient Near East, about 2100 B.C. Metropolitan
Museum of Art

With awakened interest in mathematics, it is believable that some artist's listening ear sensed the science of sound, and shaped this forked instrument with thin, movable disks that would resound in various tones when shaken.

The bird, a poetic addition, is perched on the topmost rung and gives, symbolically, a relationship of melodic notes to the whole design arrangement.

Musical instrument. Bronze. Height 13 inches. Near East, about 2000 B.C. Metropolitan Museum of Art

Carved strokes sweep across horns and heads and backs of the animals in this design; shorter strokes mark out, methodically, sections of their bodies. The legs make repeated, bending bands and the feet form a strip, almost a base-line border.

A large eye, slightly down-cast, and a young one wide open lend feeling to the design, and a thought that the protector is a shelter and the protected one is safe.

Antelope with young. Carved soapstone. Near East, Hittite, 1000 B.C. Detroit Institute of Arts

It is interesting to compare these two designs. The bronze deer of 2000 B.C. was molded by a man of primitive culture who intended it not as an art object, but as an offering to the good spirits who might help him get his food. He made much of the antlers so as to designate exactly the kind of animal he hoped would be in his path when he went hunting.

The camel was made centuries earlier, but by an artist of higher development. It shows a conscious knowledge of decorative quality. And the silhouette as a whole expresses emotion, the artist's sympathy for a sad, humped-up beast of burden.

LEFT *Figure of a standing deer.* Bronze. Iran, 2000 B.C. Metropolitan Museum of Art
RIGHT *Statuette of a camel.* Bronze. Iran, 8000 B.C. Metropolitan Museum of Art

There is a startling effect sometimes in the lines of a geometrically shaped figure. This piece of bronze has twisted asymmetric sides and strained angles, made by outstretched wings and the continued lines that enclose the bird's bending neck.

Rivets in the delicately chased metal show that it was once fastened to a pottery bowl, found shattered in a doorway where people had been fleeing from enemies, their house ablaze.

The design and workmanship of this bronze object are evidence of rare genius in a civilization that was conquered and became deeply buried.

Handle in shape of a bird. Cast bronze. Ancient Near East, Mannaen, 9th century
B.C. Metropolitan Museum of Art

Neighboring countries were usually enemies. Sometimes races and nationalities came face to face for the first time when war captives were brought in chains. These enamel plaques show an artist's interest in types that were excitingly strange to him.

With keen discernment and careful design, he has described national characteristics of faces and apparel unknown in Egypt. There, the physical appearance, the customs and the art had been developing in isolation for thousands of years.

Series of glazed tiles. Foreigners in Egypt. Egypt, time of Rameses III. Museum of Fine Arts, Boston

LEFT *Pottery bowl with slip decoration.* Egypt, pre-dynastic, about 5000 B.C. Metropolitan Museum of Art

RIGHT *Pottery cup with white band on dark slip.* Crete, pre-historic, 2200–2000 B.C. Metropolitan Museum of Art

DESIGN OF ANTIQUITY

from the springs of genius
— Egypt, Greece

EGYPT

Egypt, shut into her Nile Valley, developed an art that was the expression and simplification of unspoken religious beliefs—the prayer for protection of mortals by the gods, the promise of eternal life.

This hand of yellow glass is designed severely. It has three taut lines of fingers and a curve of palm and thumb.

Inlay: hand of yellow glass (ceremonial). Egypt, Ptolemaic, exact date unknown. Metropolitan Museum of Art

Lotus flower. Glazed pottery. Egypt, 1375 B.C. Metropolitan Museum of Art

Straight lines and a curve were enough to form the cup of the lotus, that mystical flower sacred to the Egyptian gods. Within the dark cup, petals of the blossom are seen, marked to point upward radiantly.

More freely drawn in a rhythmic row, lotus petals border the top edge of this vase. Lower down they are spread into a circular design, beautifully adapted to the form they cover.

Endless ways were found to express in design this sacred flower, symbol of the river Nile, giver of abundance.

Vase with handle, lotus petal decoration. Egypt, 18th dynasty. Metropolitan Museum of Art

House near the Nile. Wall painting of garden. Egypt, about 1250 B.C. Metropolitan Museum of Art

The artist who made this design had seen the spread and thrust of things that grew at the rich, damp edges of the Nile. But care has been taken to give each plant a decorative design of its own. Even the gardener and his dog have their place in the bends of the arrangement. Only the clean lines of the house are straight and solid. The base of the column represents in design the growth of the papyrus plant.

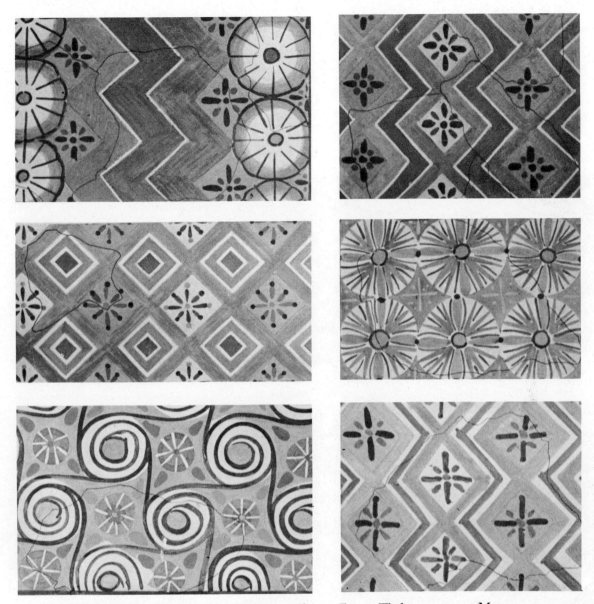

Painted ceiling patterns, from tomb of two sculptors. Egypt, Thebes, 1400 B.C. Metropolitan Museum of Art

Rooms of tombs where the walls were covered with pictures sometimes had the ceilings painted in simple geometric designs. The units in them were measured and placed exactly. But they were never tight and mechanical because of the freehand strokes of the brush, and no two were alike.

Contrasts of light and dark were brought out strongly in some places, subdued in others. Such patterns had life.

LEFT *Artist's sketch of Lion*. On limestone. Egypt, Thebes, 18th dynasty. Metropolitan Museum of Art

RIGHT *Artist's sketch, profile of Sen-Mut*. Egypt, Thebes, 18th dynasty. Metropolitan Museum of Art

LEFT *Trial sketch of a sparrow*. On limestone. Egypt, Thebes, 1400 B.C. Metropolitan Museum of Art

RIGHT *Trial sketch of a capital*. Limestone. Egypt, 18th dynasty. Metropolitan Museum of Art

On long Egyptian days, out in the sun or in dimly lighted tombs that were being decorated, these "trial sketches" were made on handy scraps of limestone. One artist drew a limber lion. One experimented with a portrait. Another caught the strut of a sparrow. The balanced construction of a capital based on the lotus was planned by a man with an interest in architecture.

Leather worker. Reproduction of a wall painting. Egypt, Thebes, 18th dynasty. Metropolitan Museum of Art

A freely brushed-in figure, such as this one, is seen occasionally among the more detailed Egyptian wall paintings. The drawing is free, but the spacing, the arrangement of light and dark, and all the moving lines in it are carefully designed.

The head settles into the shoulder line; an extended arm, a knee, a foot, all hold the long back in balance. The whole oblong space is designed—and with economy, with ease.

A bearer of gifts. Detail from a tomb painting. Egypt, 18th dynasty. Metropolitan Museum of Art

Every beautiful and useful thing that would be needed by Egyptian rulers when they ended their earthly lives and passed into the next world was represented by pictures on the plastered walls of their stone tombs. Servants as well as food and precious objects were included. But the greatest gift—discovered by archaeologists on the walls of tombs—was to future generations: the superb Egyptian design that has never been surpassed.

The design here is chiefly expressed in the erect head and extended arms. They are made with simple masses of tone, marked with flowing outlines that lead to and surround the glowing urn.

Section of wall painting. Tempera on plaster. Egypt, Thebes, 18th dynasty, about 1580 B.C. Metropolitan Museum of Art

Two boy attendants, confident of the gifts they bring, offer sacred lotus flowers and a dinner of ducks. Here again, it is the design of the painting that gives enjoyment.

Reaching angles are made by the arms and legs. The design they make is accented by dark skin tones. Long feet, which were customary in Egyptian designs, hold the figures firmly to the ground line.

Heads and legs were always drawn in side view, torsos and eyes turned toward the front.

A jackal-headed deity leading the deceased by the left hand. Chapter XXX B in the Book of the Dead. British Museum, London

Since life after death was of great concern in Egypt, pictures that explained the journey of the dead Pharaoh's soul were painted on sheets of papyrus and put into his tomb. It was believed that the jackal-headed god, Anubis, took charge and gave safe conduct.

Here, the soul and the god stride across a section of the long papyrus sheet, their arms in positions that indicate forward motion.

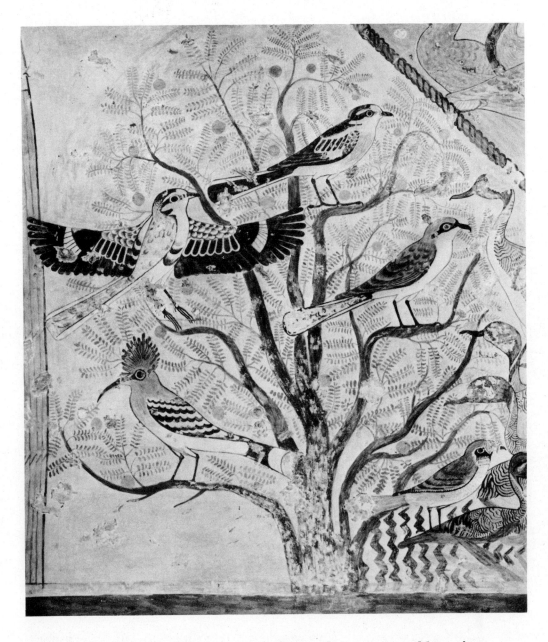

Fowling scene, from a painting in a tomb. Egypt, about 1900 B.C. Metropolitan Museum of Art

Egypt was a land that survived like the old tree in this picture, washed by the floods of the Nile, putting forth the same decorative leaves, welcoming the same kinds of birds. But endless repetition of ideas in their work stifled the inspiration of designers, and finally, the Egyptians were left in shadow by the brilliant originality of the Greeks.

GREECE

Seal stone for printing an impression.
Greece, Melos, 7th century B.C. Metropolitan Museum of Art

The Greeks were the first people to experiment in self-government. Freedom made them like a new race, free to praise, free to criticize and free to use imagination. They were original in their art because they were original in their thinking.

The flight of the bird on the seal stone above and the soaring winged horse on Athena's shield at the right seem to forecast the eventual glory of Greece.

Greek spirit and confidence were high. Life was important. Art expressed life's significance and its beauty. In the shield design, each thrust of action, each delicate stroke in the detail, shows the consciousness of beauty so extremely alive in early Athens.

Detail from an amphora; shield carried by Athena. Greece, 5th century B.C. Metropolitan Museum of Art

Mother with goslings. Terra cotta. Greece, 5th century B.C.
Metropolitan Museum of Art

Humor in small everyday matters, tenderness and leisurely observation are evident in this roughly formed little Greek terra cotta.

The sculpture at right expresses the mood of a nymph who
broods on her love for Dionysus, the Greek god of the vine.

She wears the graceful Greek chiton fastened at the shoulders.
Its folds move upward and combine with the rippling waves of the
hair that arches forward, making an enclosure for the dreamy face.

Detail of marble sculpture, Maenad head. Roman copy of a Greek work done in 5th century B.C. Metropolitan Museum of Art

Vase, black-figured pottery, head of a horse. Greece, Athens, 6th century B.C. Metropolitan Museum of Art

In the proportions of Greek vases there is something unquestionably right—the relationship of neck, shoulder and foot, as the parts are called. This is true, whatever the type of vessel. The one above, a typical amphora, is egg-shaped with narrow neck and two high handles. The painted design is placed at the fullness of one side and is in the free, black-figured style.

Vase, red-figured, Eos pursuing Kephalos. Greece, Athens, 470–460 B.C. Metropolitan Museum of Art

In this vase the painting technique is in reverse of that on the vase at the left. The background was painted a glossy black, leaving the figures in the color of the clay. It is the red-figured style. Interest is created by the motion of curved and angular design shapes.

Red-figured kylix, game of kottabos, by the Master of the Gigantomachia. Greece,
Athens, about 500–480 B.C. Seattle Art Museum, Norman Davis Collection

This exceptionally beautiful two-handled bowl has a lively decoration at its center. Two young men are shown playing an after-dinner game popular in Athens, the object of which was the skilful toss of a few drops of wine at a distant target.

The two figures, stretched out on a banquet seat, give dashing action to the design with their reaching arms, their turned heads; with the folds of bordered robes and the stripes on pillows.

Circling the decoration is the key border, a finishing touch much loved by the Greeks, and one most often repeated, even today.

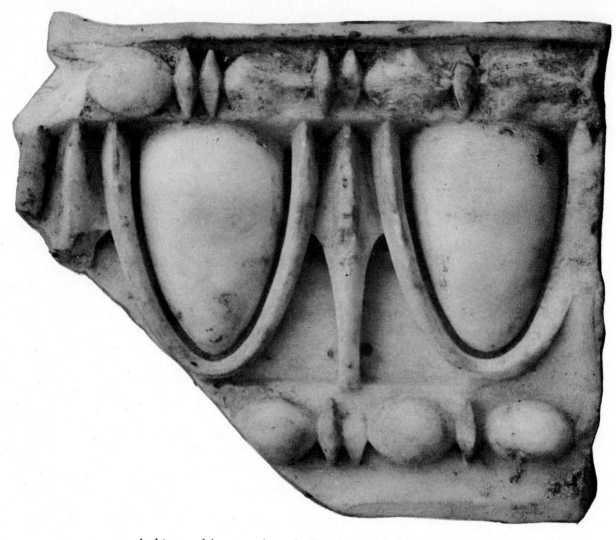

Architectural fragment from the Erectheum. Marble. Greece, Athens, 5th century B.C.
Metropolitan Museum of Art

Perfection was the standard of the Greek builders, a standard apparent in this fragment even after centuries have passed.

The bead and reel, the egg and dart, with marks of the marble-cutter's accurate hand, reflect in their small way, the perfection of a Greek temple.

Detail of Ionic volute. Marble. Greece, 5th century B.C. Museum of Fine Arts, Boston

This carved scroll, coiling inward by measured degrees to a center, is a volute. It was the decoration used on capitals of Ionic columns, and the beauty of it has affected the architectural design in many lands.

In the graduations of the curve, the Ionic volute has been found to be mathematically exact.

Fragment of marble relief, boy playing lyre. Greece, 5th century B.C. Museum of Fine Arts, Boston

There is a pleasant mood of relaxation in the design of this sculptured ornament. The player appears to have settled himself and is idly strumming the first notes of a song in praise of the gods. Lines of the composition emphasize this idea. Their long directions, angles and curves carve out lines that are consistent throughout.

A detail on the seat is exactly like the Ionic volute shown on the preceding page.

The thorny acanthus leaf was used in later Greek architecture of the Corinthian period. Its lush folds formed design much more elaborate than the designs of early Athens, where plant life was never used as a basis.

Acanthus leaves, detail. Marble. Greece, Athens, 4th century B.C. Metropolitan Museum of Art

Relief figures, Dionysus and Ariadne. Bronze. Greece, 4th century B.C. Metropolitan Museum of Art

Marble, terra cotta and bronze are the only materials used by the Greeks that survived the devastation of wars. But in these relics, the Greek devotion to beauty is evident.

Here the swirling lines and the swing of the figures tell of the romance so vivid to the Greeks in the lives of their gods.

Relief figure, Aphrodite. Bronze. Greece, 4th century B.C. Metropolitan Museum of Art

Dignity and poise and incomparable charm still linger in the design of this bronze fragment. Fires of battle did not destroy the grace of the silhouette and the refined delicacy of the figure.

Ideals lived on but Greece had fallen to her enemies. Soon another part of the world was taking an important place in design—the Orient.

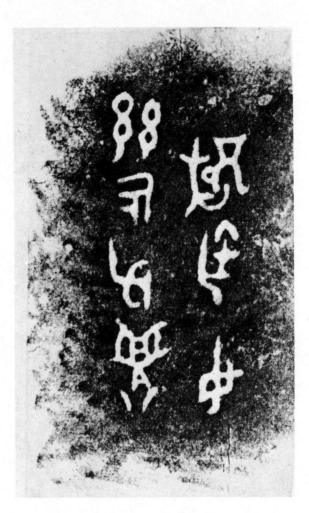

Rubbing made over a bronze inscription. Ink on paper. China. Museum of Fine Arts, Boston

ORIENTAL DESIGN

the Far East
– China, Japan

CHINA

In China little was known of classical Greece. But like the Greeks, the Chinese had the love of beauty deep in their natures. Poets chose each word they wrote for its delicacy of thought; artists strove to express, not their own personalities, but their personal and enlightened view of the beautiful.

Beauty of design could be shown in a painted cloud on a porcelain jar, a flower embroidered on silk, even the difficult shaping of a swallow in bronze on a ceremonial cup.

Ceremonial wine cup. Bronze. Height 10 inches. China, Shang dynasty, 1766–1622
B.C. Metropolitan Museum of Art

The design of the pagoda is like the verses of a poem, stanza after stanza. In construction, the pagoda is one house built on top of another, each with its own roof and its own balcony. The decorative charm of the design is shown in this large pottery model.

Looking at it, almost anyone would wish to enter such a structure, climb from one floor to another, pass through unexpected doors, look out of oddly placed windows.

Wide eaves to shelter walls from rain, a wide street doorway facing south according to custom, and delicate ornamentation of the whole façade; these are things that tell us of a Chinese aspiration— to enjoy the harmonies of life and to express them in design.

House model of polychromed pottery. Height 52 inches. China, Han dynasty, 206–222 A.D. William Rockhill Nelson Gallery of Art

Ceremonial covered vessel in the form of an elephant. Bronze. China, early Chou dynasty, or earlier. Smithsonian Institution, Freer Gallery of Art, Washington, D. C.

Chinese designers liked to express the grace peculiar to many animals. The elephant was a favorite. The patience, endurance and steadiness in his nature were appealing, but it was the gigantic proportions of his frame that pleased them most.

This bronze elephant, actually little more than half a foot high, is made to look monumental because the small one on his back is dwarfed in comparison. Designed symbols on their hides could be enjoyed by guests at ceremonies.

Two views of a statuette: figure of a man with a bear crouched on top of a pole. Bronze. China, Chou dynasty, late 6th–5th century B.C. Smithsonian Institution, Freer Gallery of Art, Washington, D. C.

The design of this bronze statuette, shown twice so we see two different views, has comedy in every line. The flip of the hand, the swish of the coattail; the way the feet seem to dance—all are as funny as the triumphant face. Even the bear seems to wiggle comically in keeping his balance. The man's motions can be imagined. They would be in short, sweeping curves.

Curves seen in Chinese design have lift and grace.

Collar from a set made for Imperial dolls. Silk. China, Ch'ien-Lung period. Textile Museum, Washington, D. C.

Certain curves of contour occur so often in Chinese design that their particular character becomes familiar. The curves that outline this collar enclose a shape that has a very Chinese deftness and sweep.

There is a similarity of curving contours in the glass vase, an object of exceeding elegance and dignity. Slight ridges follow, in harmony with the sides, down to the base which flares gently and has a rippling edge.

Glass Vase, white; translucent. China, Sung dynasty, exact date undetermined. Smithsonian Institution, Freer Gallery of Art, Washington, D. C.

Detail of a textile, fabulous animal. Silk. China, Ming dynasty, 1368–1644 A.D.
Metropolitan Museum of Art

Rippling, flowing lines often appear in Chinese fabrics. Here they accompany the movement of this fabulous beast on its way in a hurry.

Even when the old Chinese seemed most serious and grave about their mythical animals, there was often a touch of humor.

Detail of silk and gold fabric, leopard on rocks. China, Ming period, early 17th century. Textile Museum, Washington, D. C.

The fierceness of this gold leopard becomes fancifully delightful. He has been given spots shaped a little like clover leaves, and in the background, harmonizing with the body's outline, there are some wisps of cloud forms that had pleasant meaning to the Chinese. They wave smoothly and trail off. Their motion was said to suggest "the harmony of all life."

Ornament, deer and doe. White jade.
China, Ch'ien-Lung period, 1736–1795 A.D.
Metropolitan Museum of Art

A gift, in China, always contained symbolic significance. This piece of jade had not only an expression of sentiment in its shape, but special importance was attached to the stone. Jade was believed to confer all noble virtues on the recipient, especially faithfulness.

A Chinese embroidery might be entirely covered with decoratively designed symbols. Leaves, flowers, the sun, a charm, a jug with a stopper, an interlaced endless knot—all represented the treasures of ideal existence.

Such a gift had a thousand messages. Some were sacred, some were secret. Interpretation was a leisurely pleasure.

Mandarin square, embroidery (quail insignia). China, Ch'ing dynasty, 17th century A.D. Metropolitan Museum of Art

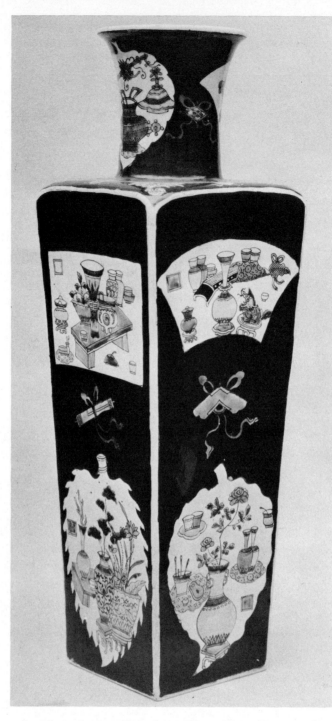

Vase, decorated with cartouches. Porcelain. China, K'ang-Hsi period, 1662–1722 A.D. Metropolitan Museum of Art

The Chinese would consider their time delightfully spent finding meanings in each tiny drawing seen through the cartouche openings on this stately vase. The use of outlines, filled in with color, was a Chinese style, which originated in woodblock printing.

Bowl. Porcelain with deep-cut key pattern. China, K'ang-Hsi period, 1662–1722 A.D. Metropolitan Museum of Art

On this bowl, another typical Chinese design is used. Straight lines are fitted together geometrically like a puzzle, covering a surface with even texture.

This style of Chinese design and many others were copied by China's appreciative followers, the people of Japan. But the Japanese eventually developed their own thoroughly original arts.

JAPAN

Boxes, part of a marriage set. Lacquer. Japan, 1622. Metropolitan Museum of Art

Japanese artists made porcelain, textiles and other things in faithful imitation of the Chinese. But there was always a difference, however slight. On the box above, the carving in the lacquer was made to swerve diagonally, unlike Chinese ornament which was carefully balanced.

In drawings and prints the greatest difference exists. Japanese pictures were not always of gods and dignitaries, but many were of and for ordinary people. Some, like the one shown here, were made on cheap paper and were sold on the streets.

Painted drawing of a dancer. Artist's name unrecorded. Japan, 17th century. Museum of Fine Arts, Boston

Bamboo, attributed to Hokusai. Ink on paper. Japan, period between 1760 and 1849. Metropolitan Museum of Art

An interesting Japanese development was the study directly from nature as it was seen in their gardens. Here is a sensitively made ink drawing of bamboo placed at the edge of the paper in an especially Japanese way.

Tops by Zeshin Shibata. In lacquer on silver paper. Japan, period between 1806 and 1891. Metropolitan Museum of Art

Design, completely imaginative, is shown in this picture where arrested motion stirs the observer's reactions—perhaps a feeling of poised uncertainty, a brief moment.

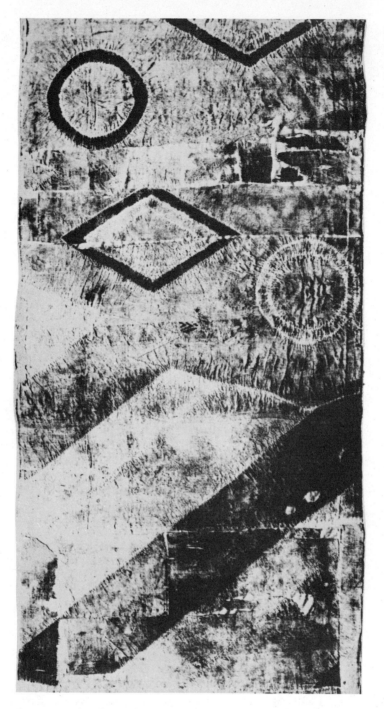

Fragment of a flag. Silk, tie-dyed. Japan. Textile Museum, Washington, D. C.

Angles are dramatic in design. Here, the dark diagonal band, agreeing with the slant of angular diamond shapes, gives this very old banner its marching pride and glory.

Robe, theatrical. Silk, embroidered. Japan, 18th century. Metropolitan Museum of Art

This costume, used in the Japanese traditional drama, has angles in its woven silk. Diamond shapes, some glowing, others dark, make a diagonal pattern. In detail, each diamond shows two facing cranes with feathers spread.

Panel, tie-dyed and embroidered. Japan. Metropolitan Museum of Art

The Japanese, with unlimited patience, contrived new embroidery stitches to add gradations or contrasts or brilliance to textiles. This panel has little framed pictures worked into the design. In a purely Japanese way, the picture details extend until they are chopped off at the edges, leaving the remainder to be imagined.

Okimono in form of a raven, by Munesuke. Hammered steel. Japan, 18th century, period between 1688 and 1735. Metropolitan Museum of Art

There was a kind of wisdom expressed in this knowing little bird, a self-contained originality.

Japanese designers wisely departed from the influence of China and made a unique contribution to the design of the eastern Orient.

In the more southerly Orient, India added her distinctive riches to the story of design.

Detail from a pile rug. India, 17th century. Museum of Fine Arts, Boston

ORIENTAL DESIGN

*along the caravan routes
– India, Persia, Turkey*

INDIA

Section of an illustration. Pindapatra Avadana. India, Nepal, 1716. Museum of Fine Arts, Boston

Legends and stories reaching deep into history appear and reappear in India's art. This illustration of the eighteenth century shows figures carefully separated but with their motions related. The gestures of hands, the tensely held heads, costumes with ornament, especially stripes—these are elements that pattern Indian designs and make them unique.

Clusters of foliage spreading out with evenness, yet each having its own variation, make places where little figures hide and are more imagined than seen. This is a decoration with the mood of poetic India.

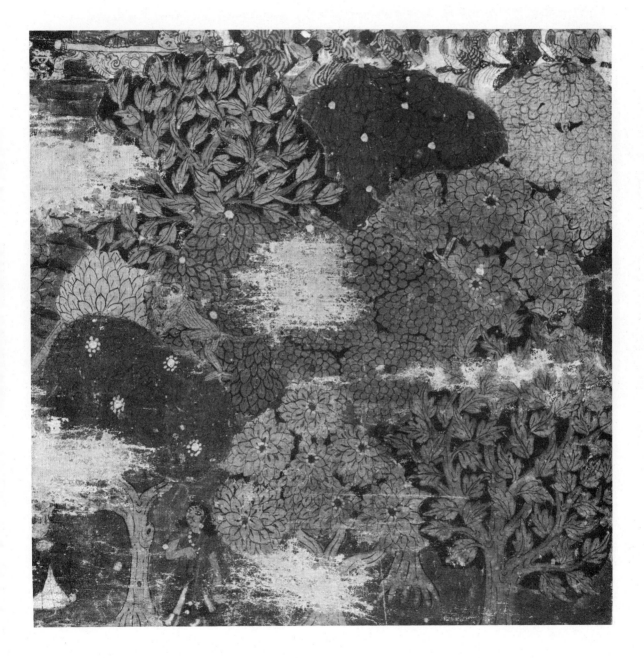

Detail of a wall decoration, deities in niches. India, early 18th century. Museum of Fine Arts, Boston

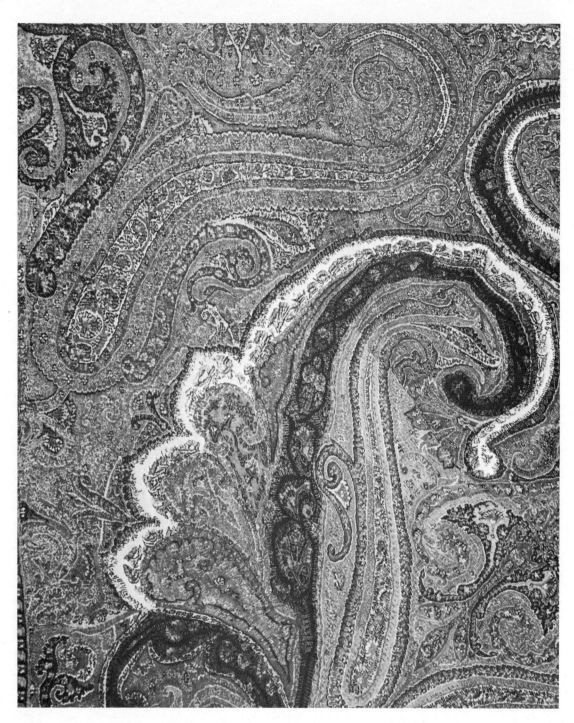

Detail from a shawl. India, 19th century. Cooper Union Museum

This Indian leaf design with its sensuous curve and curling tip is known and loved the world over. It found its way into Scottish shawls, called Paisley, where its elaborations cover wide surfaces as they do here.

Cotton cloth, painted and printed. India, 17th century. Cooper Union Museum

Familiar everywhere is this gracefully spreading tree design with details so delicate and so numerous that they may be endlessly discovered. Such intricate printing was especially beautiful on soft Indian cottons.

LEFT *Cotton cloth, cypress trees, printed brown on white.* India. Textile Museum, Washington, D. C.
RIGHT *Design unit from a printed cotton.* India. Textile Museum

Genuinely sophisticated designs are often remarkably simple. This was true of India's cottons. Here on display are examples that delighted the design-conscious people who made and wore them.

Designs were applied to textiles by various methods. They were embroidered, stamped with inked wood blocks and sometimes painted with brushes directly onto the fabrics.

The printed cypress trees above have a wood-block stroke that goes around and crosses at the bottom. Tree branches were made by angled cuts in the block. Such details are simple. The spacing of the shapes made a firmly held border.

Embroidered border on a turban. India. Textile Museum

Painted design on white textile. India. Textile Museum

Spacing can create a certain feel of being just right. The spots on the turban border at the left, each surrounded by a tracery of stitches, have sweeping curves reminiscent of Chinese design but the order of their placing is truly Indian.

At the top of this page is a painted design with no order, but full of imagination. Animals and birds hop about; trees and flowers of Indian fancy spring from strips of earth to make a lively arrangement. The artist's manner of making points by an extra flip of the brush on leaf ends, is a way of giving individuality to the design.

The pointed unit (top center) suggests the art of Persia.

Detail of border on printed cloth. India. Textile Museum

PERSIA

Carved panel from a building at Nishapur. Stucco. Persia. A copy at Metropolitan Museum of Art

Persia was a Mohammedan country. Under the rules of that religion artists were forbidden to use any form of nature in their designs. Stiffly conventionalized leaves were allowed, since they were not actually leaves but shapes.

The designer of this carved panel made the shapes of leaves bending like young sprouts emerging still unfolded from the ground.

Wood block used for textile printing. Persia, 17th or 18th century. Cooper Union Museum

Human figures in art were prohibited except when the finished work was for an important personage. This wood block printed powerful lines, angles and masses that show a man of high station helmeted and holding a scepter.

Satin brocade, made with silk and metal threads. Persia, 16th–17th century. Textile Museum, Washington, D. C.

The human figure in art was said to be sacrilege but people could be represented in designs by flowers. Perhaps some artist fancied these modest garden pinks to be people standing stiffly in obedience, conventionalized and flat.

"Kubatcha" jar. Glazed faience. Persia, 18th century. Metropolitan Museum of Art

Conventionalized also, and very important, was the shape of the Mohammedan mosque. Light traceries of its form are seen on this jar. They are like the bulbous sides of the dome and make in each case a pointed arch or ogive.

TURKEY

Curtain, linen embroidered in silk. Turkey, 17th century. Metropolitan Museum of Art

The same arching shape forms the all-over plan of this sparkling Turkish design, radiant and jewel-like.

On the right, a more regal design has flattened leaves and a pomegranate beautifully simplified.

Brocaded velvet. Ogive design with pomegranate. Turkey, late 16th century. Metropolitan Museum of Art

Textile strip, satin. Design contains Arabic script. Turkey, 16th century. Cooper Union Museum

Bowl, glazed pottery decorated with Kufic script. Persia, 18th century. Metropolitan Museum of Art

During the sixteenth and into the eighteenth century, decorations made with the Arabian Kufic script often replaced completely the representation of nature in design. The whole Middle East and even a part of India were affected by the Mohammedan rule. Art, as aesthetic experience, was stifled by the conventionality of it. But Asiatic art was moving—spreading, for better or for worse, into the continent of Europe.

Design on a Persian Wall tile.

INTERNATIONAL DESIGN

the westward move to the
European nations

SPAIN

Four tiles forming two medallions, lustre ceramics. Hispano-Moresque, 17th century. Cooper Union Museum

Eastern design entered Europe by an unexpected route. Mohammedan Moors crossed over from North Africa and invaded large areas of Spain. They were followed by other Mohammedans from the Middle East bringing their taste and their culture.

Oriental silks and tapestries had been brought to early Christian Europe by returning travelers. But by the eleventh century Persians, Turks and Arabians combined their skills on Spanish soil and established a Moorish style known as Hispano-Moresque. It was based on geometric forms.

Woven textile, compound twill. Hispano-Moresque, 14th or 15th century. Cooper Union Museum

"Interlacery" is a word that describes Moorish designs made with straplike lines, each unit helping to form another above, below and to the sides of it. Such a design has radiance, but artists grew restless with the coldness of this art. They yearned to put the forbidden earthly life into their designs.

"Drink! Live!" were the words of a very old toast. Eight centuries before this tapestry was made, they were inscribed in gold on a plate found recently in the catacombs of Rome. The same zestful pledge seems echoed in this tapestry design.

That a pledge was being made with one accord is shown most emphatically by the design. The duplication of figures, their gestures, and the balanced curves in the draped robes, all go to express agreement.

It is a strange, unique and wonderfully woven fragment. It has Moorish strapwork crossing between the roundels, but the Islamic rule against the human form in art was ignored.

When, at last, the Moors were driven out of Spain, the truly Spanish design lived again. But the superb taste of the Moors remained, as well as some Moorish blood in Spanish veins.

Tapestry, silk and metal threads. Hispano-Moresque, 13th or 14th century. Cooper Union Museum

Spain's own special genius is shown in the rare objects of tooled leather and beautifully designed ironwork. Quickly and surely we link them with history and romance.

This stout tooled leather chest, in our imagination, tells of the contents it once held—exploration maps drawn on parchment.

An iron chest, made with crossing bands tightly riveted and with locks of unyielding iron, recalls a day of galleons arriving with strongly protected Spanish treasure.

LEFT *Trunk, tooled leather*. Spain, 18th century. Hispanic Society of America
RIGHT *Treasure chest, entirely iron*. Spain, 16th century. Hispanic Society of America

Door knocker. Iron. Height, about 16 inches. Spain, late 15th or early 16th century. Hispanic Society of America

Castles in long-ago Spain had heavy doors and on them heavy knockers. The design of this one is typically Spanish in the elegance of its swift fandango curves.

Section of a gate. Wrought iron. Spain, 17th century. Metropolitan Museum of Art

There was similarity between the designs in Spanish wrought iron and the designs on textiles. In this gate, as in many iron balcony rails and stair balustrades, the orderly pattern of curling details is not unlike those in a woven cloth.

The brocaded velvet on the right has arabesques of that kind and also flower forms put there in admiring imitation of Eastern design.

Velvet and gold brocade. Spain, 16th century. Hispanic Society of America

Satin damask textile. Spain, 17th century. Cooper Union Museum

East and West meet in friendly compatibility in the spirit of this design. The two top corners show coiling wisps that are unmistakably Chinese. Persian and Spanish flourishes combine to make a design of rich splendor.

Glazed tile. Hispano-Moresque, 15th century. Hispanic Society of America

A deep mark had been left on Spanish design by the departed Moors. The few strokes that here suggest towers on a rocky coast washed by sea waves bring seductive thoughts of Spanish castles. But the balance in the drawing and the fine glaze of the tile were an artistic touch of the Moors.

And that art of glazing traveled still farther—into Italy.

ITALY

Madonna and Child. Stucco painted and gilded. Italy, 15th century. Metropolitan Museum of Art

Stucco, used for modeling attractive Italian figures, would take no glaze. Artists painted the soft surfaces, sometimes with details of Eastern design, as seen on the costumes of the figures above. But both stucco and terra cotta needed protective finish.

Glazed terra cotta bust by Giovanni della Robbia. Italy, Florence, early 16th century. Metropolitan Museum of Art

A most durable glaze for terra cotta was originated by Luca della Robbia. His nephew used it when he made this Saint John, designed in a formal manner generally seen in marble busts of the time. But the chemical formula for the glaze fell into disuse and became lost.

Then Italian craftsmen were attracted to a new process of preparing and glazing clay into wonderfully fine pottery. It was acquired from Spain. The Moors had learned the method in Asia Minor.

Pharmacy vase. Majolica. Italy, Venice, 1480. Metropolitan Museum of Art

The new pottery was called majolica, after the Spanish island of Majorca where the Moorish workshops were. In Venice and Faenza jars to hold herbs and drugs were made of majolica because of its durability. Their decorations were coats of arms or likenesses of noblemen whose patronage helped the makers of majolica to succeed. Here a patron was complimented by being given a stiff-necked, invulnerable appearance.

Two-handled jar. Majolica. Italy, Florence, early 15th century. Metropolitan Museum of Art

Majolica soon rose from the stage of mere practicality and was made to add beauty to Italian homes. On this jar, abstracted leaf forms were fitted into circular motion, radiating from one of similar shape which stands as a center. The design has Renaissance life and vigor.

Terra cotta, a frieze detail. Etruscan, 3rd century B.C. Metropolitan Museum of Art

Renaissance Italian designers were original but they were aided by many outside influences. In ancient times trading ships had come to visit the Etruscans on the west coast and their artists had remained to have a definite influence on decorative ornament. Egyptian artists had contributed details of palm and lotus that can be seen on this terra cotta slab. Then Rome had brought home Athenian architectural design to be copied.

Window, marble with iron grating and wood frame. Italy, 15th century. Metropolitan Museum of Art

Italian artists sometimes used classical details with exquisite taste. Here, beautifully carved in marble are three borders, each completely different. The inner one is the bead and reel, the next is geometrical and the outer one resembles the Corinthian acanthus leaf used by the late Greeks.

These influences were second nature to Italian designers when the more exotic designs from the East made an entrance in Italy.

Textile strip. Satin. Italy, 16th century. Cooper Union Museum

The Italian design woven in the textile on the left moves in swirls showing details of Eastern origin, the mythical griffin and the phoenix, also the coiling stems and pointed flowers of India or Persia.

Italy's design with its original warmth and its purpose of simple enjoyment, as shown below in a piece of majolica, later became overly ornate. It lost feeling. And then the artistically sensitive French took the lead in European design.

Panel of an inkstand. Majolica, Giovanni Maria. Italy, Castel Durante, 1500. Museum of Fine Arts, Boston

FRANCE

Section of the sixth unicorn tapestry, wool and silk with silver thread. France, 15th century. The Cloisters, Metropolitan Museum of Art

French genius of the Middle Ages designed and wove the most superb tapestries known today. The seven that relate the hunt for the mythical unicorn, each about twelve feet high, were made to cover the walls of a castle in southwestern France.

The unicorn is shown captured before the castle of Queen Anne of Brittany, a small segment of which is reproduced above. Tapestry shades and shadows form its towers and the windows that offered a view of the event for onlookers. Foliage enfolds the castle walls, flags fly—romance, imagination, beauty.

Section of the third unicorn tapestry, Call to the Hunt. France, 15th century. The Cloisters, Metropolitan Museum of Art

In this small detail, a perfect design is made by a young man's curving horn, his swaying costume and shouldered spear. It communicates the exciting activity of the romantic hunt.

LEFT *Detail from the sixth unicorn tapestry*. France, 15th century. The Cloisters, Metropolitan Museum of Art
RIGHT *Detail from the second unicorn tapestry*. France, 15th century. The Cloisters, Metropolitan Museum of Art

Close views of the unicorn tapestries show a profusion of foliage. A squirrel discovers a nut in a bower of hazel leaves. Pheasants rest on the rim of a fountain surrounded by plants.

In all design, foliage and flowers represent the joys of living. This was especially true of French design.

Wallpaper designed in a style from India. France, 1760–1765. Cooper Union Museum

In one more century, fine, soft cottons from India had reached France with their delightful floral patterns. French artists did not hesitate to copy the designs of twining vines that put forth imaginary varieties of leaves and blossoms, making here an Oriental garden on a French wall paper.

Button made in commemoration of early balloon ascensions. France, about 1785.
Cooper Union Museum

Whatever the French artists touched became a thing of beauty.
The first balloons were no exception. The varnished surface of the
silk bag was given decorations by most skillful designers. Every cord
and tassel helped to express the jubilation over the new invention.

Textile hanging, satin brocaded with silk chenille. France, 18th century, Louis XV. Metropolitan Museum of Art

Sometimes the French flair for decorations brought designs that were lavish rather than organized. Here a free, almost bushy effect was the result.

Textile, woven silk. Rococo design style. France, early 18th century, Louis XV. Metropolitan Museum of Art

Excessive flourishes characterize Baroque design. It became popular early in the seventeenth century and prevailed over most of Europe, creating a free, exaggerated style of decoration.

Baroque, at the time of Louis XV, was given the name Rococo, expressive of frivolous court graces. A Chinese porcelain maker received a strange order from the West and faithfully sent this bulb pot in Rococo style to France.

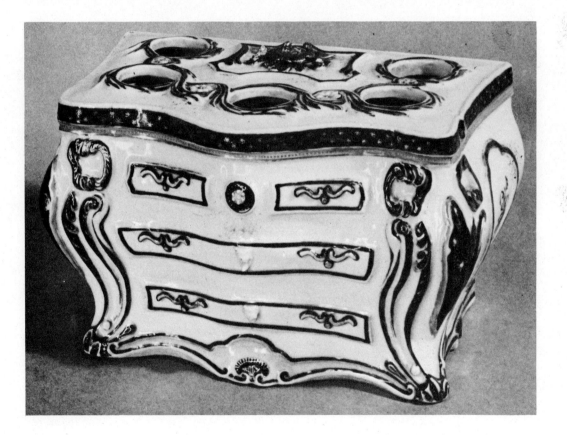

Bulb pot, porcelain, made in shape of a French commode. China, about 1765 (for export to Europe). Cooper Union Museum

Wallpaper, design of swags and a cameo. France, late 18th century, Louis XVI. Cooper Union Museum

During the reign of Louis XVI the design style was completely reversed. Patterns were composed in vertical rows. Curved lines were delicate and rigid. This wallpaper and the tiles on the next page show controlled balance of that kind.

124

Panel of twelve tiles, balanced floral design. France, 18th century. Cooper Union Museum

Wallpaper with border, Empire style of design. France, 1810. Cooper Union Museum

Once more a drastic change of design was made in France. With the arrival of the Napoleonic Empire, another style was originated. The Empire style had an imposing air in some of its details, such as the heavy draped swags that border the top of this wallpaper, the cord and large tassel.

The dress of the woman, her chair and the pitcher on the table, all are in formal Empire style.

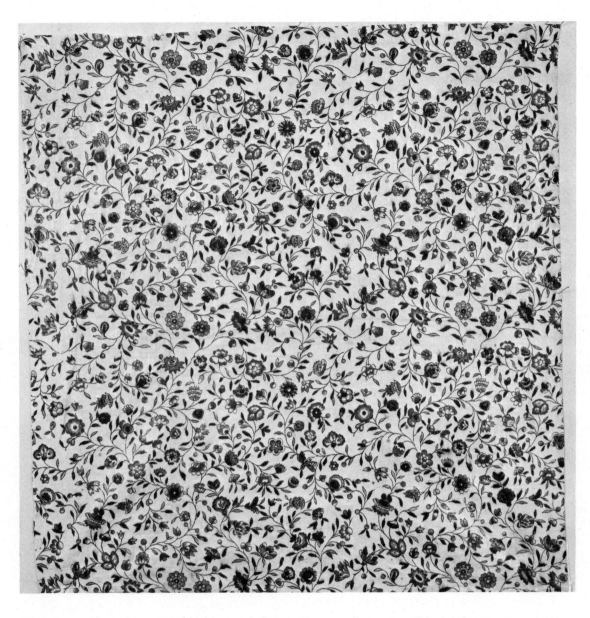

Drapery textile, cotton with block-printed design. France, about 1800. Metropolitan
Museum of Art

In the Empire period rigidity of design was lessened a little by
the use of block-printed cottons strewn with flowers. France and
flowers were inseparable and the flavor of India's imaginative botany
was not forgotten, as can be seen in the print above.

It is to the credit of the French designers that they were able to
follow many whims of taste. A more conservative and less capricious
country lay to the north—England.

ENGLAND

Bench, box-top seat style. Oak. England, early 16th century. Metropolitan Museum of Art

The English liked to use good sound sense in things they made. They had great aptitude for construction, especially in wood.

Fine northern oak for wall panelings and furniture inspired the English cabinetmakers. In the sixteenth century they were called "joiners," although they were designers as well. An example of furniture made during the sixteenth century was this seat that also served as a chest. Its ends were notched at the floor line to form legs and a carved panel nailed to the front was the only decoration.

Stool, made with four braced legs. Oak. England, early 17th century. Metropolitan Museum of Art

In the Elizabethan age, seats were no longer chests, but oak stools with legs skillfully turned in a sort of keg shape. Strong stretchers near the base held them solidly in place. The wood was oiled to a deep brown.

Hardy Englishmen, even in suits of armor, could sit on such benches and do them no harm. The design pleased because it was so right.

Wood-block printed paper, lining of a Bible box. England, 16th–17th century. Metropolitan Museum of Art

This design is in a squared-off arrangement that resembles the plan of English wood paneling. The units of fruit, flowers and nuts have interesting wood-block character and fit their spaces with ease.

Linen, with a type of silk embroidery called black work. England, late 16th century. Metropolitan Museum of Art

Here, too, the plan is geometric but stiffness is avoided by the curving borders around individual units. They differ in size and manage to fit tightly, keeping uniformity in over-all tone.

Part of panel, embroidered in wool. England, 17th century. Cooper Union Museum

Imagination gained freedom when design styles of the southern Orient reached England. Winding patterns of India, with birds, animals and swirling leaves, cast their influence on textiles made in England for wall panels or chair backs. They were full of little surprises.

Stumpwork embroidery, with historical details of Charles I. England, 17th century. Metropolitan Museum of Art

Entertainment combined with decorative quality pleased the English taste. England had the theater and great books that recounted history with liveliness. Here a moment of history and romance is put into a design.

Cleverly textured everywhere, it has islands, on four of which stand a king, a queen, their castle and a doleful singer. In the foreground is a shepherdess bringing a flower to the outstretched hand of a shepherd who is lonely among the woodland animals.

Church pew with mother and sons. Salt-glazed stoneware. England, 18th century.
Metropolitan Museum of Art

In design, this piece of mantel pottery consists only of three figures evenly placed in a church pew. But it has humor and is precious as an example of fine English salt-glazed stoneware.

Volute from a choir stall. Carved wood. England, late 15th century. Metropolitan Museum of Art

The church carvings of England were as fine as any in the world. This one has beauty and religious meaning.

There is a circle within a circle made by a ropelike vine. Small underdeveloped sprays follow it decoratively at even distances. The inner vine encloses full-grown leaves and grapes protected at the center. Detailed but not elaborate.

Doors made for 1 Portman Square, London, by Robert Adam. England, second half of 18th century. Metropolitan Museum of Art

Rhyton by Wedgwood. Black basalt. England, Staffordshire, 18th century. Metropolitan Museum of Art

The English architect, Robert Adam, advanced the Greek influence which was affecting much of Europe in the eighteenth century. These doors, perfect geometrically and ornamented only with bands of fluting around the panels, are an example of the Greek simplicity that came into vogue for interiors and furniture.

Josiah Wedgwood followed the trend with his pottery of basalt that recalled the poetic dignity of Greek vases.

Chair by Chippendale, Chinese style fretwork. Mahogany. England, 18th century.
Metropolitan Museum of Art

Trade with the Orient brought a wave of interest in the products
of China that came in sailing ships to European shores.

English designers and the owners of English homes were capti-
vated by the Chinese teakwood, the lacquer and the embroideries.

An English-Chinese style of furniture was created by the designer,
Thomas Chippendale. One of his chairs, shown above, has fretwork
in the Chinese style on back and arms. The straight, squarely cut
legs were the first of that kind to be made in England.

LEFT *Dish, painted porcelain.* China, about 1735. Metropolitan Museum of Art
RIGHT *Teapot, painted porcelain.* China, 1736–1795. Metropolitan Museum of Art

China's ports were busy shipping orders to the West. Porcelain was the export in greatest demand, particularly in England.

There was so much pleasure in using the Chinese porcelain every day that tea drinking was cultivated and tea-time became an established custom in English homes.

England's great genius was a feeling for home life. This was reflected in her ability to colonize, to rule and to protect.

Across the sea, England established her standards of home-making in a new land—America.

Part of a needlework sampler, signed "Martha Wheeler, 15th September." England, 18th century. Victoria and Albert Museum

Wooden tub, called a "piggin." Colonial America. Metropolitan Museum of Art

DESIGN

in earliest America

COLONIAL AMERICA

There have been many instances in history when the arts of new-comers to a land have become combined with those of the natives, resulting in a mixture of styles. These cornhusk dolls seem to represent an interchange of tastes between two races—the red man in a fringed rawhide shirt and feathers on his head, his wife in the costume of a colonist, both in moccasins. But no permanent blending of styles in design came about on the North American continent.

The English newcomers had deeply grounded traditions. These settlers increased in number until English colonies covered the Atlantic seaboard.

The colonists learned a great many useful things from the Indians, but English taste remained unchanged.

Cornhusk dolls, a man and a woman of Seneca tribe. America, New York area.
Museum of the American Indian

Carved panel from an oak chest, sunflower design. Colonial America, 17th century.
Metropolitan Museum of Art

The colonists were people from England's middle class, strong,
competent and filled with eagerness to make their new land home-
like.

This carved design with its three circular flowers and central
stalk took careful geometric planning. Curved embellishments fit
their spaces neatly.

But the sunflower is not a poetic theme, as the rose or the lily
might have been. It is a bright and hardy blossom, truly colonial in
expression.

Chest of drawers, carved panels. Oak. Colonial America, 17th century. Metropolitan Museum of Art

A bit of decoration gave a home a cheerful look, however rude the house might be. Even in the 1600's, when colonial life was difficult, skilled English artisans found time to carve hard New England oak in pleasing patterns.

The design on this chest front was made perhaps from memories of church carvings in old England.

Bedspread detail, made by Mary Breed. Wool on linen. Colonial America, Boston, 1770. Metropolitan Museum of Art

The desire for cheerfulness in a home on the New England coast, where winters were long and cold, must have been the motivation for this design that speaks of balmy days. A great variety of stitches were used to make the gently waving branches with eleven decorative birds and the clover at the tree's roots.

Reading and writing chair, Windsor type. Colonial America, 1700. Cooper Union Museum

The Windsor became an American chair, although it had origonated when an English wheelwright conceived the idea of fitting "spokes" into a curved railing that he made into the back rest and arms of a chair. It was a clumsy tavern chair when it came to America. The wheelwright's idea was improved upon. Lines were lightened, legs were slanted strongly into the seat and the chair from the region of Windsor Castle became an American fireside chair.

Carpet, made by Elizabeth Stowell. Wool. Colonial America, 1790. Metropolitan Museum of Art

Slat-back armchair, maple and ash combined. Colonial America, 1725–1750. Metropolitan Museum of Art

Simplicity, by the time the colonies were a century old, was natural to the way of life in the new world. Little effort was spent on ornamenting the "slat-back chair." Sturdiness was the virtue of its strongly joined woods and rush seat. Slats slightly bent and arms curved as rests were enough for comfort.

The rug shown on the left, with its design of repeated arches, has an unostentatious charm.

Then, as conditions changed, so did design ideals become changed.

Marble plaque with carved spread eagle. United States, 18th century. Cooper Union Museum

DESIGN

in the new nation

THE UNITED STATES

Bald eagle design, inlaid wood. United States, New York, 1796–1810. Metropolitan Museum of Art

The bald eagle had been chosen as the national bird. The stars and stripes had become the symbol of freedom. A new mood, a new self-esteem among the people, brought changed taste. Simple things like plain wood chairs no longer satisfied. Only the finer English styles seemed suitable to homes in the proud capital cities of the young nation.

This chair, made expertly in America, copied the curving top edge and the straight, square legs of the English Chippendale. Upholstery came into fashion, and ornamental textiles such as this one showing George Washington and Benjamin Franklin mark the patriotic Federal period of design.

Wing chair, upholstered in printed cotton. Mahogany. United States, 18th century.
Metropolitan Museum of Art

Exceedingly fine workmanship went into the making of American furniture. Designs of Robert Adam and his contemporaries were copied with only slight alterations. This chair has the shield back and the spade foot of the English Hepplewhite style.

The old Windsor chair underwent still more refinement. A number of different woods were combined in a single chair, each for its particular strength or beauty. Grace and a fine polish brought the Windsor into American parlors.

LEFT *Armchair, English Hepplewhite influence.* Mahogany. United States, 18th century. Metropolitan Museum of Art
RIGHT *Windsor chair with "comb back."* Four woods combined. United States, 18th century. Metropolitan Museum of Art

Bedcover, made entirely of wool. United States, Connecticut River Valley, 1796. Metropolitan Museum of Art

In this beautiful piece of needlework, marked 1796, the design has the feel of India and Persia in the flowers. There is even a Chinese teapot. All together it makes the kind of design that England had produced with adaptations from various countries and now passed on to America.

Wallpaper on a bandbox, a fashionable design. United States, Philadelphia, about 1835. Cooper Union Museum.

It was fashionable in the 1800's for women to carry bandboxes. Wallpaper was made in strips of special width to cover them gaily. The design above represents an estate garden with pheasants proudly spreading their feathers. The spaces in the design are very cleverly arranged for purposes of dash and smartness.

Pieces of pressed glass, clear and colored. United States, Pennsylvania, 19th century. Metropolitan Museum of Art

American ingenuity created a substitute for costly glassware by pouring hot, liquid glass into molds the way cast iron and bronze are made.

This "pressed glass," sometimes called Sandwich glass because the first of it was made in Sandwich, Massachusetts, toned up American dining tables. It was either crystal clear or chemically colored, and the designs were generally in imitation of fine European cut glass.

Stenciled decoration on a plastered wall. United States, New England, post-Revolution. Century House, Watkins Glen, N. Y.

Artists who might have created a really American design found no natural niche for their talents where only English taste was considered right and proper.

Perhaps creative ability could have been found among the young men who traveled the roads of New England carrying their kits of paint and stencils with which they decorated the plastered walls of farmhouses in return for meals and places to sleep.

Their patterns, such as the one above, gave a touch of decorative beauty, even splendor, where they were used over mantels and along wall edges. These designs are collected and cherished today.

England lost her colonies in America, but her customs, her taste, her energy and her standards of craftsmanship remained influential all the way from Canada down through Florida. Things made on the Atlantic Coast were carried across the plains to the Pacific. But the English colonies were not the whole of America.

Today a wider range of design can be seen. It includes the contributions of the almost unnoticed colonists who came to America as early or earlier than the English—the Spanish, the French, the Dutch and the Scandinavians.

Bell tower of church. Quebec, 1815.
By Baillargé, architect and carver.
Provincial Museum of Quebec.

DESIGN

of the forgotten colonists

Not all the first settlements of European people in North America allowed their tastes and customs to be controlled by England. They made homes to their own liking, and the design which was characteristic of each nationality was preserved.

Things made by those half-forgotten colonies have enriched American design as a whole. Beginning with the most northerly of the settlements, we have New France, later to become French Canada.

Small cupboard of natural pine. (Pottery from School of Quebec). French Canada, Montreal. Provincial Museum of Quebec, Paul Gouin Collection

NEW FRANCE

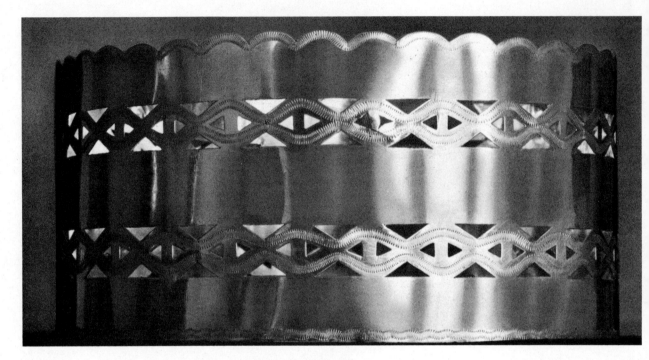

Silver crown, made by Joseph Tison, worn by an Indian Chief. Canada, Montreal, 1787–1869. Provincial Museum of Quebec

New France, north of the St. Lawrence River, had become a British possession in 1763. And while it is said that French people always remain French wherever they are and under all conditions, yet these French colonists departed from European tradition to some degree and used originality in their arts.

The design of this plain silver crown has a combination of straight lines and curves that express brilliance in a superbly simple way.

LEFT *Silver cup, made by Jean François Landron.* Canada, Quebec, 17th century. Provincial Museum of Quebec
RIGHT *Silver plate, made by Jacques Pagés.* Canada, Quebec, 1710. Provincial Museum of Quebec

This cup has only a small amount of design detail. Its beauty is in the graceful contour. The silver plate has a simple radiating pattern where rhythmic ridges catch the light.

Buffet of natural pine. Length 4 feet, 6½ inches. Canada, Quebec, about 1790. Provincial Museum of Quebec

Beauty is here enhanced by what has been omitted, by the amount of open space in relation to design details. This buffet is French in feeling, but the simplicity and the scraped pine of which it is made are characteristic of French Canadian originality.

Cock, a chimney cowl, made of plate iron. Canada, vicinity of Montreal, 1720. Provincial Museum of Quebec, Paul Gouin Collection

Although Canadian designers were original, they retained French spirit and French sentiments. A favorite figure in their design was the cock, Chanticleer, from the old fable. Here he is seen made of burnished and painted iron. He was placed high on a church roof with his comb standing erect like a little crown and his neck arched as if he were crowing to announce the dawn.

In such things, the traditions of France lived on in the region along the St. Lawrence.

Not far distant from the French colony was another vigorous group of settlers, the Dutch, at the mouth of the Hudson River.

NEW AMSTERDAM

Two panels of a cookie mold. Wood. New Amsterdam, 17th century. Museum of the City of New York

In 1653 the Dutch named their colony New Amsterdam. The colonists built windmills on their farms and some little gabled houses along the crooked paths of Manhattan Island.

The most homey and sociable parts of the Dutch houses were the kitchens. Things made for them were designed to combine usefulness with good cheer. The carvings on the cookie mold above and on the spoon rack at the right are lively and decorative in design.

Spoon rack with ornamental wood carving. New Amsterdam, 17th century. Museum of the City of New York

NEW YORK

Carved wood panel showing Dutch colonists. New Amsterdam, 17th century. Museum of the City of New York

In only a few years New Amsterdam was claimed by England and renamed New York. Life became more prosperous. People dressed well; homes were patterned after the fine architcture of Holland.

Beautiful furnishings were in demand, and silver from which to make tableware was plentiful. Some of it had come to New York in the form of Spanish coins to be melted down for re-use.

Silver porringer by silversmith John Hastur. New York, 1726. Museum of the City of New York

Young people, taught by master silversmiths from Holland, became extremely proficient. Designs were dictated by custom for their usefulness. This silver bowl has a handle that was usual at the time, flat and shaped like a crest, but it was in Dutch taste.

The Dutch of New Amsterdam laid claim to a small colony settled by Scandinavians on the Delaware River. But the English, insisting that their grant included this region forced out the Swedes, the Norwegians and the Danes and took the entire territory for themselves.

171

THE NORTHWEST

Panel from an altarpiece, woodcarving by Lars Christensen. United States, Minnesota. (Photo courtesy of the National Gallery, Washington, D. C.) Norwegian-American Historical Society

Although New Sweden on the Delaware had lasted only sixteen years, the Scandinavians had no intention of giving up their settlement in the new world. They simply moved on into Wisconsin and Minnesota where their familiarity with forest life and their skills as builders and woodcarvers were reflected in the homes and churches they built.

Altarpiece panel, woodcarving by Lars Christensen. United States, Minnesota. (Photograph by Wangsness) Norwegian-American Historical Society

Immigrant artists may have received European training, but this man's designs show an earnestness about life in the new country, about having a home and a church that would compare favorably with those anywhere. And there is originality and feeling in that fine protective curve around the figures.

Handicraft pattern. Norway, Oslo. Designer, Halfdan Arneberg

Patterns to be stamped or embroidered on cloth were brought by immigrants from the Scandinavian countries. This lively one with fashionable people and a village scene expressed an ideal close to the hearts of pioneer women.

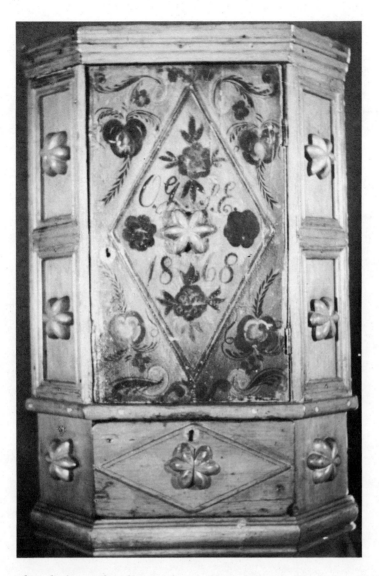

Corner cupboard of carved and painted pine. United States, Minnesota, 1868. Private collection of Marion John Nelson

To make much of little is an aptitude among Scandinavian craftsmen that forms a background for their design of today. To know materials, to prepare them well and to design with simple, conservative charm is a Nordic quality noticeable in this little cupboard, made by an early Scandinavian American.

In the Southwest, a less fortunate colony suffered conquest by Indians and struggled with poverty. They were the Spaniards who had come from Mexico and who had bravely held their ground at Santa Fe.

THE SOUTHWEST

Candlesconce. Tin, stamped with tooling dies. United States, New Mexico, 1800's. Museum of New Mexico

Since silver for craftwork was not to be had in the Southwest, artists used the only metal available. It happened to be tin; not sheet tin but scraps of lard and oil containers that came there over the Santa Fe trail from the East. And the beauty created was Spanish.

The design of this tin candlesconce harks back to designs of old Spain—the tooled leather and the wrought iron. The style was instinctive, the workmanship adapted to conditions in the Southwest.

Candlesconce. Tin, punched with nail and chisel. United States, New Mexico, early 1800's. Museum of New Mexico

Candlelight gleamed along the radiating bends of this circular reflector, carefully soldered to the very Spanish wing-shaped parts above it and below.

The Spanish taste, the Spanish flair, were in the natures of these New Mexican artists, some of them descendants, perhaps, of Florida colonists who had found life easier in Mexico. Missionary trails led them north out of Mexico into the American Southwest.

Trastero, or cupboard, made without nails. Pine. United States, New Mexico, 1700's. Museum of New Mexico

Great capability for building with accuracy is evident in this cupboard, held together by mortice and tenon construction. There is marked Spanish character in its appearance, especially in the design of the doors.

Wall hanging, solidly embroidered with wool yarns. United States, New Mexico, about 1850. Museum of New Mexico

Zigzags can be found in the designs of most every country, beginning with Egypt. But here the scalloped edges and the little inset triangular details have a Spanish character. And when this embroidery is imagined on an adobe wall, it belongs, beyond all doubt, to the American Southwest.

Tapestry designed by Henri Matisse; woven by Gobelin. France. French Embassy
Press Information

DESIGN

in the contemporary evolution

PRE-HISTORY
and TODAY

This story of design began with pictures of small carvings made thousands of years ago in Northern Europe. From the same part of the earth come these recent carvings made by a skilled designer. There are similarities and there are differences.

More efficient tools are used today, and greater skill. Surfaces gleam from careful polishing. But the two groups have one thing in common. The crude little bear and bird of amber on page 7 were designed spontaneously from the artist's own feeling, with no rules to follow. The same is true of contemporary design.

Birds of the Northland: ptarmigan, tern, penguin. Carved from whale bones by Arne Tjomsland. Norway, contemporary. Norwegian Information Bureau

FORM, FEELING
and DESIGN

Here, the idea of basing a design on a feeling of natural forms has achieved abstraction in interesting ways.

Marks in the weaving—a coiled line and an almond-shaped spot that resembles a shell opening—are the slight details that show how thoughtfully natural construction has been considered. The four units fit rhythmically together. They are shell shapes, but the design is almost completely abstract.

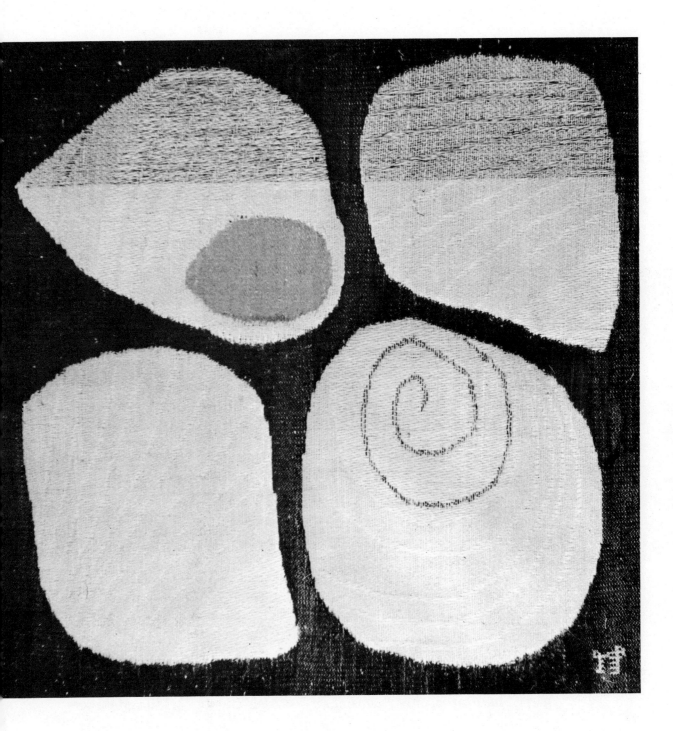

Square panel, woven by Dora Jung. Finland, 1958. Cooper Union Museum

CONTOUR

A sensitive hand and a sophisticated eye can mold clay into contours that are simple, subtle and of lasting interest.

The form of this vase, lightly squared, slightly graduated downward, is not mechanically exact. Instead it retains the artist's touch, telling the motions that shaped its contour.

For decoration there is a medallion with a single spray sketched on like brush writing. It is the famous artist Hamada's customary way of signing his work.

Pottery vase by Shoji Hamada. Iron rust glaze. Japan, Mashiko, contemporary. Craft Horizons

LINE

The "line," as the term is often used, is the current or direction in an art creation that dominates the design. Often that line, that indication of direction, determines the beauty as a whole, especially in the work of contemporary artists.

In this glass there are contours with long, clean edges, followed by shadows and by reflected lights. They echo one another, slip smoothly over each other. Together, they accentuate the feeling of undulating line that was in the artist's original conception of the design.

Group of glass vases by Arne Lindass. Norway, Oslo, contemporary. Norwegián Information Bureau

MOTION

The motion in this design may have been suggested to the artist by a memory of some swiftly beating action or with the feeling of imagined earth layers folding slowly, each with its own texture.

Whatever the initial source of a design idea, the observer's interpretation depends greatly upon his own experiences to add vividness of impression.

Tapestry, woven of wool, silk, cotton, by Pamela Stearns. United States, 1962.
Museum of Contemporary Crafts

STILLNESS

Some of the most beautiful contemporary designs convey, not motion but repose, an almost mystifying stillness. It is true of this triple panel.

Fascination with these glowing rectangles of glass develops and increases through close examination. Some of them are alone in their places, some are fused with other kinds. A few are brilliant, others subtle and subdued. Dark ones are often surrounded by an edge of light, and all are held firmly in position by a rough texture made of minute particles.

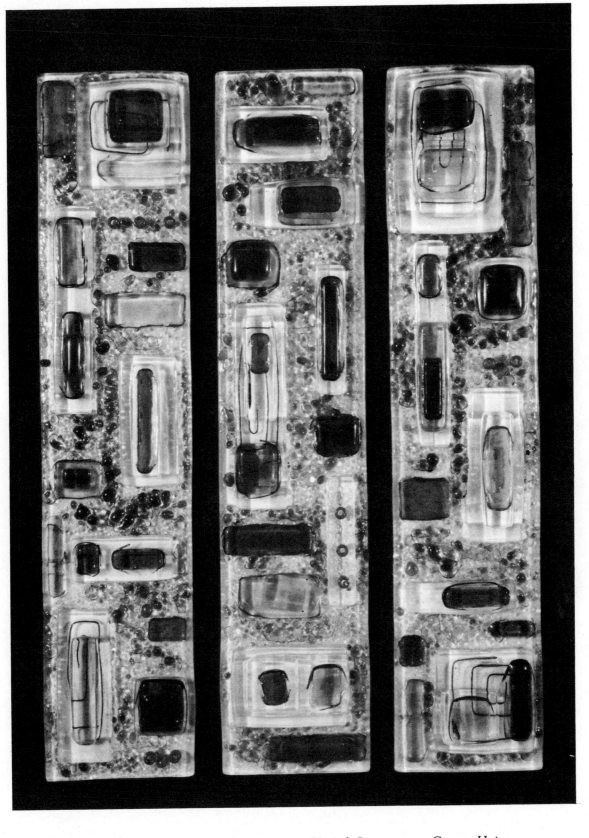

Triple panel, fused glass, by Dorothy Larson. United States, 1959. Cooper Union Museum

SPACING

The area of this tapestry has been spaced exactly into thirds. But the important part of the design is made by the details, each one a clever little design in itself.

Although these details are spaced to carry out a superimposed pattern, their arrangement is not purely mechanical. On close observation, they seem to have been placed by hand in a way pleasing to the artist.

Tapestry by Prof. S. Galkowski. Poland, Cracow, contemporary. Polish Folk Crafts and Art Center

PRACTICALITY

Chairs have changed through the centuries. Comfort has become more important than grace and ornament. Durable materials and serviceable proportions fill modern demands for practical living.

Curves that accommodate the human form, legs that brace strongly and safely, length of frame that allows for informal, half-reclining positions are all characteristic of modern chairs. And they have their own kind of sophisticated attractiveness.

Large armchair designed by Gio Ponti. Italy, contemporary. Centro Italiano di
Informazione

FAMILIAR MATERIAL,

UNCOMMON USE

Contemporary designers sometimes find unusual and inspired uses for materials. Wood for a lampshade would have been thought impractical until it was successfully used on the perpendicular sides of this tiered lamp.

The wood is so thin that over light bulbs it is translucent and the grain shows. The lamp's glow is soft and mellow.

Lamps made entirely of wood. Designer, Hans Agne Jakabsson. Sweden, contemporary. Scandia Crafts

AGE-OLD,

BUT NEW

A frame of poles with an animal skin fastened over it made a hammock-like seat in homes of the Vikings. Today a chair based on the same idea is daringly contemporary.

The carefully shaped oak frame is balanced on legs that are angled to support weight. Sheepskin, wooly side out, is cut to a pattern and stretched on in straplike fashion. It forms a deep seat, a back, and arm rests. Inventor, the Vikings.

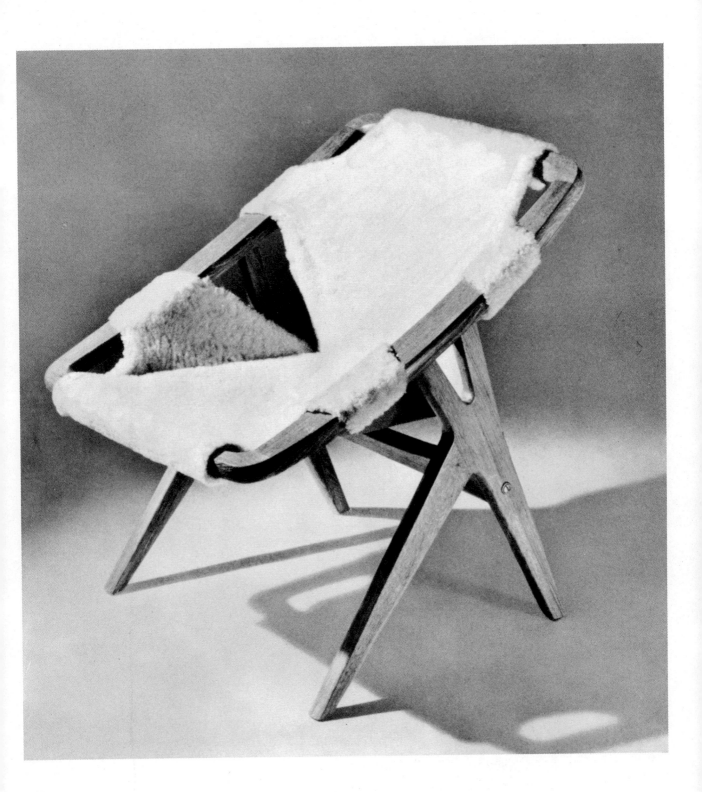

Armchair covered in sheepskin. Designer, Arne Tidemand Ruud. Norway, contemporary. Scandia Crafts

STATIC HARMONIES

This design needs no title. Meaning can be read into its non-objective blocks of tone that seem to build upward with the many horizontal bars. In its static blocks there are astonishingly near and far effects. But modern harmonies of rectangular space divisions, however rigid, are its intent and purpose.

Carpet designed by Maria Laszkiewicz. Poland, contemporary. Polish Folk Crafts and Art Center

SPONTANEITY

Brush strokes made with perfect freedom have the charm of the artist's own touch. On this fine porcelain they have a quick, almost playful spontaneity. But the brush has followed the forms of the objects with design sensitivity.

The pottery and the decoration are casual in style but masterly in craftsmanship.

Ceramics. Denmark, Copenhagen, contemporary. Danish Information Office

IMAGINATION

Imagination creates designs and it also contributes to the enjoyment of them. The orderly pattern shown here arouses that instinct.

Things in nature are sometimes partly seen and partly hidden. Filtering light in a forest will touch some of the foliage for a moment. Darker places wait, half lost in dimness.

Such imagining discovers the charm of this textile. Bright threads make illuminated details. Tones of dark make quiet rows in the over-all horizontal effect.

Wallpaper designed by Gerald C. Papia. United States. Birge Company

MYSTERY

An artist's meaning in a design is not always obvious. Happily it is often left for conjecture, and sometimes is enveloped in mystery.

These vases with shaded swerves in the glass seem to offer, perhaps, a chance to look deeply beyond the present, to envision some beautiful dream, out of reach but glowing with the promise of possible attainment.

This fine contemporary craftsmanship presents design experience; strangeness that is intriguing.

Crystal vases by Mona Morales-Schildt. Sweden, contemporary. American Swedish News Exchange

TRADITION

In a few parts of the world tradition is revered more than original-ity and newness. This is true of India where the creators of beauty in modern times are deeply sure of the rare elegance in the designs that are their heritage, and continue to follow them.

Even the toys made of clay or wood or paper are seriously designed and reflect the artists who fashion them. The little figures shown here, with their contrasts of white cloth and dark skin, are like the figures on some of India's oldest printed cottons.

To be contemporary in art is a matter of choice.

Craft toys made in a village workshop. Balsa wood. India, modern times. India's Finest, Importers

ABOVE *Glass vase by Hermann Bongard.* Norway, contemporary. Norwegian Information Bureau

BELOW *Pottery ladle from Zggouries near Corinth.* Greece, 1400–1150 B.C. Metropolitan Museum of Art, Gift of the Greek Government

Design today is a new, fresh expression of moods and impulses that have always lived deeply in human nature. Design today has its own character, but when, as quite often happens, a design that is thousands of years old is found to measure up proudly with those now called contemporary, the present seems very close to all yesterdays and the future only another link in the long, enduring chain of the world's design.

SELECTED BIBLIOGRAPHY

(Many of the books listed below also include specialized bibliographies)

AARS, FERDINAND. *Norwegian Arts and Crafts.* Dreyers, Oslo, 1957.

BEAZLEY, JOHN D. *The Development of Attic Black-figure.* University of California Press, Berkeley, 1951.

BLOSSFELDT, KARL. *Art Forms in Nature.* E. Weyhe, New York, 1929.

BRACKETT, OLIVER. *English Furniture Illustrated.* Macmillan, New York, 1950.

BYNE, ARTHUR. *Spanish Interiors and Furniture.* Helburn, Inc., New York, 1922-25. 3 vols.

CHRISTENSEN, ERWIN OTTOMAR. *The Index of American Design.* Macmillan, New York, 1950.

———. *Primitive Art.* Crowell, New York, 1955.

DAVIES, NINA DE GARIS. *Ancient Egyptian Paintings, Selected, Copied and Described.* University of Chicago Press, Chicago, 1936.

DOWNER, MARION. *Discovering Design.* Lothrop, New York, 1947.

HATJE, GERD. *Design for Modern Living.* Abrams, New York, 1962.

HONEY, WILLIAM BOWYER. *European Ceramic Art, from the end of the Middle Ages to about 1815.* Faber, London, 1949-1952. 2 vols.

JONES, OWEN. *The Grammar of Ornament.* B. Quaritch, London, 1868.

KOYAMA, FUJIO. *Chinese Ceramics.* Nihon Keizai, Tokyo, 1960.

LEE, RUTH WEBB. *Early American Pressed Glass.* The author, Northboro, Mass., 1946.

LION, DAISY (GOLDSCHMIDT). *Chinese Art: Jade, Sculpture, Ceramics.* Universe Books, 1960.

LIPMAN, JEAN (HERTZBERG). *American Folk Decoration.* Oxford, New York, 1951.

LIVERANI, GIUSEPPE. *Five Centuries of Italian Majolica.* McGraw-Hill, New York, 1960.

METROPOLITAN MUSEUM OF ART. *Chinese Textiles: an introduction to the study of their history, sources, techniques, symbolism and use.* By Alan Priest and Pauline Simmons. New York, 1934.

———. *A Handbook of Mohammedan Art.* The Museum, New York, 1958.

NUTTING, WALLACE. *Furniture Treasure.* Macmillan, New York, [© 1928] 1954.

POPE, ARTHUR UPHAM. *A Survey of Persian Art.* Oxford, London and New York, 1938-1939. vols. 1-6.

PFUHL, ERNST. *Masterpieces of Greek Drawing and Painting.* Macmillan, New York, 1955.

PLATH, IONA. *The Decorative Arts of Sweden.* Scribner, New York, 1948.

RAPHAEL, MAX. *Prehistoric Pottery and Civilization in Egypt.* Pantheon, New York, 1947.

RICHTER, GISELA MARIE AUGUSTA. *The Sculpture and Sculptors of the Greek.* Yale University Press, New Haven, 1930.

SCOTT, ROBERT GILLAM. *Design Fundamentals.* McGraw-Hill, New York, 1951.

SMITH, WILLIAM STEVENSON. *The Art and Architecture of Ancient Egypt.* Penguin Books, Baltimore, 1958.

STENNETT-WILLSON, RONALD ALFRED. *The Beauty of Modern Glass.* The Studio, London, 1958.

STRANGE, THOMAS ARTHUR. *An Historical Guide to French Interiors.* Scribner, New York, 1950.

THOMSON, WILLIAM GEORGE. *A History of Tapestry from the Earliest Times until the Present Day.* Putnam's, New York, 1906.

TOKYO NATIONAL MUSEUM. *Pageant of Art Series,* 6 vols. Toto Bunka Co., Tokyo, 1952.

WARING, JANET. *Early American Stencils on Walls and Furniture.* Century House, Watkins Glen, N. Y.

WEIBEL, ADELE COULIN. *Two Thousand Years of Textiles.* Pantheon, New York, 1952.

WILDENHAIN, MARGUERITE. *Pottery: Form and Expression.* Reinhold, New York, 1962.

ZIMMER, HEINRICH R. *The Art of Indian Asia.* Pantheon, New York, 1955. 2 vols.

RENEWALS 458-4574

DATE DUE

FEB 2 1			
GAYLORD			PRINTED IN U.S.A.